THE ENERGY OF ABUNDANCE

How to manipulate energy to gain abundance

Dr Hein Lambrechts

CONTENTS

1. INTRODUCTION

You have probably read a lot of books, attended seminars and bought a lot of audio courses. All of them make promises and you believed it. Unfortunately, after all your efforts, you are still in the same powerless position. All of the resources did get you excited, but even that faded away after a day or two. No results. You are still searching for that magic book...

This book will be different. It is short and to the point. It will give you the direct answer. Don't underestimate the power of these words, just because the book is cheap. It is the result of years of research and the true value of this information is priceless.

This book must end up with as many people as possible. It can make a difference in the world and the consciousness of the world. This book is written to help the people who cannot afford all the expensive books. It is also written for the people who don't have time to read a three hundred-page book. If you want to read something with more length and explanation, go and get my book, Subconscious Beliefs.

If you are serious about changing your life, read and apply this information. Your life will transform and change dramatically. All I ask in return is that you let me know of your great success you are going to achieve. I need the testimonies in order to spread the word even more!

Leave a reply or review at Amazon or kindle. You can also e-mail me at info@subconsciousbeliefs.com with your testimony or success story. (Pictures are not necessary, but it will be much appreciated)

Thanks in advance.
Enjoy the book!

2. ENERGY

It is necessary to understand how things work here on planet earth, in order to advance to the next level of your life.

Einstein used a formula that all of you are familiar with.
$E=mc^2$
Energy = mass of an object x the speed of light.[2]

What does this have to do with you?
This is not a science lecture, but if you look at the formula, you'll find that everything in the universe is made out of energy. The energy is moving so quick, that our senses create the illusion of an object.

If we should take a little sample of your skin and put it under a telescope, you'll see that your skin is made out of cells. If you look even closer you'll discover things like molecules, electrons, protons and atoms. To keep it simple – quantum science has proven that everything is made out of plain energy. It is actually more correct to say that everything IS energy. That includes the rocks and the trees – everything.

The only reason you don't appear to be energy, is because the energy vibration is so fast that you appear to be solid. Let's use an example - The energy vibration of water, ice and steam are different, but they are the same substance.

Why is this important to know?

The effect of energy in your life cannot be over emphasised. The fact that you cannot see energy doesn't mean it has no effect on you. Health and wealth are the result of energy. If you have a lack of health or wealth, it is an indication that you have an energy blockage.

If you are depressed or fatigued, chances are good that you are carrying with you a lot of negative energy.

You must remember that you are disposed to all sorts of energy during a day and at the end of a regular day, you usually have a residue of negative energy. People can tap your energy if you allow them to. Unfortunately, people are not aware of the effect of energy and how to manage their energy.

If you are not excited by now, you probably don't really understand this golden nugget of information. In short, you can drastically improve your life by giving attention to the management of your energy – no exceptions.
You CAN and WILL see results, guaranteed. It's law. It must.

You'll find that the bible makes a lot more sense, now that you know that everything is energy.

You must have heard before that we are all one? The bible shows us that you must do unto others what you want to do to yourself. If you hurt somebody else, you are actually hurting yourself.

Now you know why. If you are energy and I'm energy, then we are of the same essence. If a person is stealing from somebody else, he/she is actually stealing from him/herself!

I always wondered as a child how God can know every person on earth and how He can hear the prayers of the millions of people. Now you have the answer. God is the highest form of energy, love. We are part of that energy and that is how He knows you.

2.1 LIFE HAPPENS

Every person is energy. Right?

Every person therefore must have a certain dominant energy vibration.

These energy vibrations differ from person to person. That's why there are so many different people in the world with different results.

Here is the big secret of a successful life: The level of dominant vibration you are emanating determines what you are going to attract in life.

If you have a high dominant energy vibration, you'll attract things of the same high level of frequency, which are good things.

If you have a low dominant energy vibration, you'll attract things of the same low level of frequency, which are the not so good things.

You'll find in the bible that those people who have a lot will be given more and those who have little will have even less. Read the previous paragraph again and realise why this is so! If you have very little money, you have a low energy vibration and you will attract even more things of a low energy vibration. Change your energy vibration and you will change your life.

If things are going bad for you, it just tends to get worse, doesn't it?

In times when you are happy and enough money, everything just seems to fall into place for the better.

Your dominant energy vibration is determined by your upbringing, the beliefs you have, personality and talents you may have. The strongest vibration of them all is created by your beliefs. Yes, even your beliefs are energy.

You must become familiar with this energy concept. Even the words on this page are emanating energy.

Your dominant energy vibration is largely determined by your beliefs. Most of your beliefs are hidden in your subconscious mind. You are not aware of them.

You may have a limiting belief that money is not good for you. The most common beliefs about money are:
- I don't deserve money
- People who struggle financially are good people
- Money is bad for you/only bad people have lots of money
- It's difficult to get money, etc.

Consciously you'll disagree with me, because you are not aware of what is going on in your subconscious mind. Guess what? You'll stay broke, as long as that limiting belief is still in your life. It is sending out an energy vibration that is pushing away money.

If you are having a life of struggle, it simply means that your dominant energy vibration is attracting those things in your life.

It is almost as if we all have an unconscious thermostat. If you are not familiar with a thermostat, i.e. used to keep temperature under control. If you have an air conditioner at home and you have set the room to be a certain temperature, then the thermostat is going to help that the temperature is not going too high or too low. It will switch on and off as needed.

Our belief system works on a similar basis. It will ensure that you stay within the boundaries of what you belief. Just think of the dramatic transformation if you can change the settings of your unconscious thermostat. The good news? You can!

2.2 VICTIM MENTALITY

If you are one of those people who are blaming the world for the things that happens to you, you have a long road ahead to recovery.☺

If you want to get your life back on track, you'll have to stop blaming others, the world or anything outside of yourself. Being a victim will bring you nowhere fast. It is just an excuse for why things are not working out for you – and a reason for stop trying.

I want you to go and find a mirror. Look into it (and if you are not a vampire☺), you should be able to see yourself in the reflection. Go ahead and smile into the mirror. Is the reflection smiling back at you?

Here is the thing – you want something, a certain end result. It can be a car, house or a certain amount of money. Why do you want it? Mainly because it makes you feel good – the main reason why humans do anything.

Let's assume that the smile on your face is that end result you want, O.K?
How did you get to see that reflection of your smile? You have to smile first!

What we are doing in life is we are looking into the mirror with a somber face and are waiting for the reflection to smile back at you. It's not going to happen!

Let me use an example -I'll be happy when I have a million dollars. You are not happy now, but you belief you will be – somewhere in time.

You need to smile first, to see the smile in the reflection. You need to change yourself first, before you'll see the results. Don't wait for something to happen. DO something NOW and then expect the results.

The world is a reflection of yourself. It is a mirror of what is going on inside of you. Yes, even the terrible things that happen in the world is trying to tell you something about yourself.

You don't have money NOW, because your dominant energy vibration is repelling money. There must be a blockage in your energy vibration or your energy vibration is so low that you only attract bad things into your life.

Change your dominant energy vibration and you'll change your life. Change your beliefs and you'll change your vibration and you'll change your life.

Easy isn't it?
The difficult part is HOW do I change my dominant energy vibration?

The information that follows may seems logical, but very few actually apply these principles. The answer to your problems is so easy, you tend to miss it totally. Please APPLY these things and you WILL see dramatic results!

3. CLEAR THE ENERGY CLUTTER

The energy around you will have an influence on your own energy.
It will therefore influence the results of your life as well. It is of the utmost importance to clean the energy around you and raise your own dominant energy vibration.

Start off by cleaning your house. Take one room at a time and clean out all the clutter. Get rid of the dust and the things you don't use anymore. There is a lot of people in the world that have less things than you do and they will appreciate the things you give to them for free. If it is things that nobody will want, throw it away!

I'm not suggesting that you get rid of everything! Follow your gut feeling on this matter. You'll be surprised how good you feel afterwards. The reason you feel better, is because you got rid of the clutter energy. The room and the house will have a new feeling to it.

Remember that every little thing in this world is made of energy. All of those little things that are displayed in your house also have a certain energy vibration. It actually gets even scarier! ☺ All these things have memories, as well and memories are energy as well.

I have interviewed a lot of psychics and all of them explained to me the effect of energy. Old houses especially have a lot of memories and unfortunately most of the memories are negative. Negative memories = negative energy.

There are various ways to clean the energy of a house or even a workplace. It may be the reason why your business is struggling!

Go to http://www.subconsciousbeliefs.com and listen to the recordings of my Talk show for some advice. There is lots of advice on how you can clear the energy of your house.

A very important place to clean out is your bedroom where you sleep at night. If the room has negative energy, your subconscious mind is going to be influenced by this negative energy.

Remember that your brain waves are slowing down when you rest or sleep and therefore the access to your subconscious mind is more open.

The next thing you need to do is to clean out your own energy.

You cannot have any vitality if you consume the wrong food. The modern diet is loaded by sugar and 99% of all people are addicted to sugar. They cannot function effectively without it!

If you are one of those lucky ones who don't consume sugar, did you now that there are a lot of hidden sugars out there. Sugar even has different names on the products. This all is due to the fact that the manufacturers want to make money out of you. If they can still add sugar into the product and call it something different, the people will buy and they will still make their money.

Did you know that there is sugar in catch-up? O.k., you knew that one, but did you know that there is sugar in milk?

I think you get the idea.
You don't have to follow any diet. Just follow these rules.
Cut out sugar and see how your life changes.

Drink plenty of good quality water. Very few people do.

Remember, it is going to help you raise your dominant energy vibration!

Go on a detox and clean your body of its' blockages.

This is not a book on dieting (and by the way, don't ever diet!). My advice is to change your lifestyle.

Exercise regularly. If there is one addiction you can learn, it is this one!☺

Learn how to breathe properly. We are so occupied with out thoughts that breathing is the last thing we think about. Take a deep breath and hold the breath for as long as you can, without feeling any discomfort. Slowly exhale and repeat the exercise for at least three or four times. Your body will thank you for that.

Try and breathe more consciously. When we are stressed, we tend to breath very shallow. Unfortunately, shallow breathing has become the custom and we now need to consciously breathe more deeply. Your body will get more oxygen and you will relax more.

3.1 EMOTIONAL CLUTTER

Most people have lots of hidden emotions that accumulated throughout the years. These emotions are suppressed and are nothing other than energy that you need to keep down.

To keep down this energy you need to use your own daily quota of energy to suppress it. It takes energy to carry around unused energy.

Let's assume you start of the day with a 100% energy level. Before breakfast you have already used up about 30% of your energy due to hidden and suppressed emotions. You are carrying those emotions with you, just like a bag on your back.

Imagine how much more energy you are going to have if you can let go of your suppressed beliefs.

The rest of the day you are going to meet with people and amongst them you'll get your typical energy vampires. Energy vampires are people who is always negative and who is unconsciously tapping your energy. You are also going to need your energy for daily functions like eating, walking and running.

Can you see why you are so tired by the end of the day?
You kick out your shoes and what do you do? You eat a TV dinner (bad energy) and you watch some TV. The daily news channel seems to be interesting to you... (terrible energy).

For some reason some people seem to be addicted to bad news and pain! Just keep in mind that the only way newspapers are being sold, or the news channels are being watched, is if they give you the most sensational bad news possible.

Please put your focus on the positive. It is almost like typing in a word into a search engine (like google). Whatever you are looking for on the World Wide Web, you just type the word(s) and the search engine will give you lots of results regarding the searched item. Life works similar and whatever you focus on (the words you type into google), you tend to attract (google's results) into your world.

If you are searching for tragedies, google will give it to you. If your looking for success stories, that is what google will give back to you. Life also gives you what you are asking.

The problem however, is that we are very good in asking for bad things. After reading this book, you'll be able to use your same manifesting powers, but for attracting good things into your life.

3.2 DO THINGS DIFFERENTLY

The saying goes that only a fool will do the same things over and over and then expects different results.

You'll have to enlighten your life. BE CONSCIOUS of your energy consumption!

Identify what you need to change in your life. Some things just don't serve a good purpose in your life and may be pulling you down. Sit down with a pen and paper and try to identify what actions are not to your overall benefit. Try to avoid these things in the future.

One can only move to your target or goal or away from it. You never stand still, because everything is changing constantly. It's your decision if you are going to stay on your road to success.

Start NOW. Don't postpone, because their will never be a right time to start.

Try to do things differently than what you usual do. Perhaps you can drive to work following a new route. Spoil yourself with some new clothing or a new haircut. Eat something different and throw in a few compliments to strangers. You'll be surprised how great effect small things like this will have in your life.

3.3 FEELINGS

Feelings play a very important part of in your life and your manifestations.
Why?

The feelings you have are an extension of the energy you are vibrating to the world. If you are feeling great, you are emanating a high-energy vibration to the world and in the process you'll attract things of a high-energy frequency.

In plain English, if you feel great, you'll attract more great things into your life.

If you are feeling bad, you emanate a low energy vibration and attract more bad things into our life.

Your feelings tell you what you are attracting in your life.
The aim is to feel great every day of your life. If you have followed the advice so far and did clean the clutter around you and inside yourself, you'll probably be feeling great already!

One of the secrets of life: It is not what happens to you that matter, but how you react to it.

Attitude is really everything. Happiness is just a decision you need to make.
If you want to be unhappy about something, you'll get enough reasons to support your theory. If you decide to be happy, enough reasons to be happy will surface. Yes, it is all in your mind!

Feelings will always tell you if you are on the right track or not.

4. EFFECTIVE ENERGY MANAGEMENT

So far you have cleared all the bad energy around you and you gave started to clean out your bodily system from negative energy. You cannot reach your goals if you are always tired. By removing emotional blockages and stuck energy around you, especially the place where you sleep, will help a lot.

Eat healthy, get enough sleep, exercise and drink enough good quality water. If all of these things are not helping you, you must go see your doctor immediately. Please remember that there is such a thing as too much as well. Too much sleep will make you even more tired.

Let's see how your energy goes day-in and day-out. You start of with approximately 100% energy. This is not true for everybody. Some people will wake up after a night of little rest. This can be due to various reasons. If you still have a sibling in your home, the reason will be obvious. Perhaps you had a late night dinner, which took some time to digest, leaving your body tired.

A lot of people spend their nights worrying. Others just have a poor mattress. The reasons are endless. If you are lucky, you wake up with 100% energy. At an average, let's say that a normal person, considering all of life's' circumstances, wakes up with 90% energy. This is 90% positive energy.

The moment you are awake, your subconscious (who didn't sleep) kick in the old beliefs and habits. You'll remember that every belief is energy as well and depending on the type of beliefs, some of them can be very negative. Negative beliefs tap your positive energy.

You are not conscious of these limiting beliefs that are negative energy. It remains hidden in the subconscious mind. Eliminating such beliefs will obviously enhance your overall energy. Let's say you have a few bad habits, like eating a doughnut for breakfast. This will contribute to your energy loss. The doughnut will increase your energy momentarily, but in the longer run (a few minutes later) it is going to put your body under more stress. Stress is negative energy.

On your way to work there is a traffic jam and you stress, because you don't want to be late for work. A driver cuts in front of you and you get upset. All of these things contribute to your overall energy of the day.

Can you see why you sometimes get to work feeling as if you haven't slept? Your energy may be at about 60% by now. During the day you encounter a lot of people and some of them may tap your energy even further.

By the time you get home that evening you are literally depleted of energy. A lot of people go in the red of their energy reserves and some will even fall asleep very early.

The secret here is to manage your energy effectively. Eating the right kind of food will enhance your energy. Knowing how to handle negative people will prevent you from loosing energy. Keeping your energy high will help you attract more high-energy events into our life.

Sometimes you can have invasive energies that you are not aware of. Getting rid of these energies is beyond the scope of this book, but there are a lot of resources available to help you. If you still feel you are drained of energy after following all of these steps, invasive energies may be the cause. On my website, www.subconsciousbeliefs.com there are a few experts that you can contact for help.

4.1 LIMITING BELIEFS

Let's start with some limiting beliefs. Becoming conscious of them and replacing them with good, positive beliefs will enhance your energy dramatically.

Deborah Hill, who I was honoured to interview twice on my talk show, has written a book "Unlimited Life" in which she identifies a few limiting beliefs that has a major impact in your life and energy. People forget that they have these beliefs and these beliefs keep draining them unconsciously. By becoming conscious of some of them is really a revelation!

I'm going to mention a few that had a major impact on me.

The first one is applicable in cases where your family is tapping your energy. You can always pick your friends, but you cannot pick your family. The result of this is that you cannot always avoid family member's problems and complaints. You may feel you have a great life and the only thing bothering you, is your family and their problems!

First of all, I want to warn you about your subconscious mind. You don't want your subconscious mind to think that your family member's problems are yours. If you tend to get emotionally involve in their problems, your subconscious is going to assume that it is actually your problems it is dealing with. Try to help, but you need to keep a distance emotionally.

The limiting belief most of us have, is that we can live other people's lives. Parents must be careful in raising their kids. We obviously wants what is best for our kids, but a lot of parents try to achieve what they couldn't achieve through their kids.

I know your child is your must valuable "possession". I have two of them as well. Believe me, I'll do anything for my children and I know you will too. Just be careful not to influence your children's decisions. They have talents and interests of their own that you need to take into consideration. Don't force your interests onto them. You can still guide them, but in the direction they desire. You can't live your kids' lives through them.

The same applies to the rest of your family. If you have energy sapping family members, beware! Try and help them as far as you can, but in the end you must remember that they are living their own lives, making their own decisions. You cannot be held responsible for it, if they make some poor decisions. This obviously extends much further than family.

We tend to get so involved with other people's problems, that we forget it's not really our problems. It may sound insensitive, but you are not here to solve other people's problems!

The instructions you receive before an aeroplane takes off is that in case of emergency, you need to put on the face mask first, before you can help the kids or the elderly to put on theirs. You are of no need to others if you pass out!

The same applies here. You are still in primary school (so to speak) learning how to manage your energy. You can only start to help others if you graduate from university!
The world is full of blind people leading other blind people.
That is the reason why most people keep on struggling with their lives. You will not let a mechanic operate on your heart, will you? Why then do you listen to other people for advice, if they also have their own similar problems?

If you understand how to empower your life and you start doing it, PLEASE help others (but you still need to think of yourself first). If you are not sure how to do it, help yourself first.

Spending loads of energy on other people's problems, are not going to help your current situation if you don't know how to handle energy.

The moment I realised that I cannot own other people's problems, it was a big weight that was falling off of me. Becoming more of yourself is going to serve others and the world much better than you worrying about other people's problems.

People with problems are unconsciously tapping other people from their energy. They don't intend it, but that is what actually is happening. They are desperately trying to gain energy to deal with all their energy depletions.

Recognise it immediately. Confirm that their problem is not your problem. Obviously, you must do this in your mind and not out load!! Go ahead and give advice if you do have some advice for the person. Experience however, have taught me that those people just need you to confirm that they have problems you can do nothing about. If you start giving advice, they seldom listen or even apply your advice....it's human nature.

The moment you leave this person, take away your focus to something nice. (By the way, you don't want to stay with this person for too long.) Congratulations – you have just avoided energy depletion!

Ilene Dillon, also one of my guests on my talk show, has written a great book about energy sapping. She explained to me that it is human nature for small babies to be energy sappers. They need the energy from their parents to survive. When they turn two or three years of age and they are more independent, they usually stop the energy sapping, because they don't need it anymore. Unfortunately a lot of people didn't stop the energy sapping and they are still continuing it (unconscious of course) when they are adults.

You don't have to be a psychic to know who are "energy vampires." You'll immediately feel it. Surely you have experienced people who have a zest for life and you just want to be around them. Why? You feel alive around them! If you are not as exited as they are, you are probably tapping their energy☺.

The same applies to people who are draining the energy out of you. You just don't want to be around them. These types of people usually don't have a lot of friends. (Not always! There are exceptions).

Another limiting belief is that there is not enough time. We can start the discussion of linear time and that time doesn't exist, but I've promised to keep it short. Let's look at time.

4.2 TIME

Imagine time is a room in your house. The room has two doorways. You start your life's journey in the one doorway and you proceed through the room to the other doorway or the exit. Are you still following?

You are the one moving, not time (the room). You start with childhood and as you walk through the room you get older and you go through the phases of life. The exit presents your death.

Does this analogy help you to understand the concept time? Time is constant and it will always be there. You are the one moving through life, but time stays the same. We have just altered the concept to help us understand it better.

I'm sure you have noticed how slow time can go by if you are doing something you don't like. Time on the other hand flies when you are having fun, doesn't it? Can you see how consciousness and time relates?

If you believe there is not enough time, you'll experience exactly that. Time is a mindset. Let me explain. Life tends to fly by you if you are acting on default every day. What I mean with default is that you go through life on automatic mode (unconscious of all the moments you have). The more you become conscious, the more you'll experience that time actually doesn't fly. Remember that you always have enough time.

The biggest problem with the human race is that we get stuck in automatic mode. We stick to what is familiar and safe. If a routine can be established, even better! Why is this so?

Your subconscious mind wants to have the world figured out. It is protecting you and if something different is happening, it will immediately pay attention and try to get you back into the mode you were before. Let's look at it further.

5. SUBCONSCIOUS MIND

Your subconscious mind gained information and recorded experiences throughout your whole life. It has currently an opinion of life and of you and your place in society. All of this recorded information is now beliefs. You are never going to second guess any belief of you. Why not? Your subconscious mind created it to protect you and it is not going to allow you to tamper with it. It has already made up its' mind.

This is the reason why it is so difficult to change habits or stick to a diet. Obviously there are beliefs that are very good for you, for example the belief that fire will burn you. Unfortunately there are also limiting beliefs. That is beliefs that don't serve you. You'll agree that if you can bypass some of those limiting beliefs, you'll create magic in your life.

What about bad habits? Why does the subconscious mind allows you to get bad habits, like smoking, if you know it is bad for you?

The subconscious mind is very powerful, but it has no idea what is good or bad for you, other than what you are experiencing in your life. That is why you are attracting either good or bad. Whatever you are asking, it gives to you.

The subconscious mind only look at short-term gratification. It is always trying to avoid pain and trying to get pleasure. If you enjoy smoking, it will let you continue smoking – it makes you feel good. It doesn't know it is bad for you.

The subconscious mind also doesn't understand reason. You can logic it to death and explain to it that smoking is bad for your health, but it will not understand you. The subconscious communicates with pictures, feelings and emotions. Time for an example:

Yell some nice things to a baby and the baby will cry. Say some nasty things in a friendly tone and the baby will smile. Do you see? It was not the logic behind the exercise, but the tone of voice or feelings that determined the outcome. It is the workings of the subconscious mind.

You can use your subconscious mind the get rid of some nasty habits, like smoking. The only requirement is that you need to communicate with it by pictures, feelings or emotions.

If you can imagine (in full colour pictures) something bad happening to you when you light a cigarette (add some nasty feelings/emotions), and you do it constantly, the subconscious will get the message of pain and it will help you to quit smoking.

The only reason people start smoking again, is if they stop using the visualisation technique when they smoke, or they are used to the procedure of smoking (the way they hold the cigarette or the time they use to smoke). In such a case you'll find that it is the conscious mind that is making the decision. The subconscious mind already quitted smoking successfully, but your conscious mind is telling you it is hard to stop smoking.

The main theme and message here is that you need to take control back of the steering wheel. Your subconscious mind is like a baby that is behind the steering wheel of a car. The car has all the power, but you need someone who can steer this vehicle.

If you are in control, you can guide your subconscious mind and get some powerful results in your life.

5.1 FINANCIAL TIPS

This is not going to be a long discussion on the economy and ways to safe money etc. Just a little bit of practical thinking that can make a big difference in your life.

You'll be surprised, but many people don't budget. Starting from this moment you need to draw up a budget. Remember to budget for some unforeseen circumstances as well. See where you can cut unnecessary expenses.

Here is a little secret that alone can change your fortune. People tend to pay their bills with their paycheck, but they don't pay themselves. You MUST take 10% of your pay and put it away for yourself.

The secret however, is not to go and spend it. Save it. Originally it may seem hard to this (I know you need to survive through the month!), but you'll be surprised how you will forget about this money and still manage to get through the month.

Before you know it, you'll have a considerable amount of money that will make you FEEL like a rich person. Your energy vibration will be higher and money will come to you more easily. After you have saved nice amount of money, you can use it to invest and let it grow even further. Try it for a few months and see what you think!

I'm a firm believer that the world is what you believe it to be. If you believe this book will not change your financial position, then it will not. All I ask is an open mind. You have nothing to loose!

Believes are also energy and it WILL influence your results.

5.2 PERSPECTIVE

Remember that your life is like a colouring a picture. Life and its events are neutral (the picture). You are the one giving life meaning with your interpretation (the colouring in).

You can colour in the picture with dark colours, i.e. see all the negative in everything. You can also colour in the picture with bright, beautiful colours, i.e. see the positive in everything.

Every event is indirect neutral and it is HOW you perceive it that makes a difference in life. You can get frustrated in traffic and get to work in a bad mood or you can use the time in your vehicle productively, thinking good thoughts and listen to empowering mp3's. You'll be in a great mood when you get to your work! You see, the same situation, but a different approach.

Even your perception of your past can influence your life. Nothing stops you from changing your perception about the past and creates a great tomorrow!

Your mind loves to be in the past or in the future. It hates the present tense, because then you are in control. If it can keep you busy with worries and regrets, you are under its control. You need to live more conscious!

It is always a good idea to personalise your mind and to communicate with it. Please do this in your own private time or silently in your head or else the people may think you are mad ☺!

Imagine a funny dressed person and give him/her a name. This will be your symbol/ image of your mind. Treat your mind as this person and negotiate with your mind on a variety of things. Explain to it the benefits of your actions or else it will retaliate.

This exercise may seem strange, but the results will amaze you!

5.3 THE POWER OF THOUGHTS

At this stage you should know now that your dominant energy vibration will determine your level of attraction in your life. This is not something you can see, but you can track it by the way you FEEL. Feelings are the indicators of your level of vibration.

It is obvious that the better you feel, the higher your energy vibration will be. The ultimate goal is to have a very high vibration, since this is what attracts abundance into your life. You NEED to get excited about life again or you'll never succeed. Why do you think people start to make their fortunes when they do what they love? Because they get excited about life!

Getting rid of energy clutter and cleaning your body by being healthy are among those things that will help you raise your energy. Limiting beliefs are also blockages that are keeping your energy vibration level low as it is preventing the flow of energy through you. Remember that energy is always flowing and vibrating. It is always flowing through you and your charkas. The ideal situation is to have all your charkas open. This book is not going to discuss and explain charkas, because you don't need that knowledge to have dramatic improvement in your life.

Feelings are the indicator of how high or low your dominant energy vibration is. You NEED to get excited about life again or you'll never succeed. Why do you think people start to make their fortunes when they do what they love? Because they get excited about life!

How do you manage to stay excited about life, if life is happening and nothing seems to work out for you?!

Let me give it to you straight.

This is the answer you have been looking for your whole life. There is no "how to" solution that will fix your problems. The only solution is that you need to live your life more consciously.

Let me explain. People tend to live on default. Your subconscious mind has figured out everything it needs to know about your life (in the early years of your life). It has formed lots of beliefs and has decided where you fit into society and what you are capable of doing.

Your subconscious mind hates changes and will prevent any changes in your life. This is the reason why it is so difficult for you to succeed with diets or to stop smoking or whatever. Why?

The subconscious mind's main priority is to keep you save. If you want to change the wires in the machinery (as a figure of speech), it will immediately stop you. It wants to stick with what is familiar and save. As a result, most people start to act on default. It is the same procedure over and over every day of their lives.

Can you see why you will always attract the same level of abundance, no matter how hard you try? You are stuck in the same level of vibrational activity. You can't do the same thing every day of your life and expect different results can you?

You need to change to a higher energy frequency and that will require some changes on your part. Most people tend to wait for something to happen in order to be successful or happy. I'll buy that car when I win the lotto. I'll be happier once I get out of this relationship. I'll loose some weight if I earn more money to buy a gym membership.... There are millions such examples.

It is not surprising to see the end-result. These people will stay exactly where they are – in waiting mode. Nothing will change.

If you want something to change in your life, YOU need to make the change. It seems so logical, but very few people actually take it serious! You need to take back control of your mind.

Your subconscious mind had received so many contradicting messages throughout your life that it started to ignore you. You want to loose weight, but you also desire some junk food. Despite this, you are still the captain of your ship and you need to take control back!

Let's get back to living a more conscious life. Every moment you are living in the present moment, you are living consciously. You are aware of what is happening around you and your senses are heightened. Unfortunately, we are not in this mode for most of the day. Our thoughts tend to take over during the day and we start to act on default (you are not really aware of your surroundings, because you are in thinking mode.) Before you know it, he day is over, but you can only recall the highlights of the day (which required your full attention).

The idea is to stay conscious and to divide all your actions into different parts. You are driving your car (driver-function) – that will be one complete action where you stay conscious of what you are doing. You arrive at work (employee-function) – you focus on your work.
You are arriving home after work (family-function) – you spend time with your family talking and discussing things, without your mind focussing on the work.

If you can identify each action and stay aware, you'll start to live consciously.

Why is this so important?

The subconscious mind looks at all things and thoughts and is continuously looking at what can go wrong. The end-result is to have millions of people on earth that is very negative and always considering possible bad outcomes. You are probably also one of those people, but don't despair. This is totally normal. It is the way the subconscious mind functions and the way it tries to protect you – to have you ready for things that can go wrong or backfire on you.

So why do we want to change that?
98% of all negative thoughts and worries never happen in your life. Why spend so much time wasting your thought energy?

The average human has about 60 000 thoughts every day. 80% of those are negative thoughts. The next day, most of those thoughts are repeated. How is that for negative programming?! Can you see why your positive affirmations you do every day for 15 minutes, is not going to be able to do much about your situation?

You can repeat to yourself that you are rich and successful until you are blue in the face. Your subconscious mind is only going to think – 'Oh really? Who are you kidding?'

Have you ever decided to stop eating chocolates? Before you know it, you have eaten five chocolate bars in an hour (and normally you eat only two chocolate bars in a week!). It is just your subconscious mind showing you who are in control.

If you life more consciously, you will become aware of your thoughts that pop into your mind.

You cannot stop your thoughts – and that is not the goal behind this. You just need to become aware of your thoughts.

The thing of thoughts is that they can influence your emotions. The ideal situation is to have good emotions. Here is a neat little trick you can use if you realise you are falling into the bad emotions:

Think of the best place in the world that you just love. Imagine it in detail – see it in your mind's eye... Let's say you just love it on the beach. Be specific: Hanauma Bay in Hawaii? Do you feel the sun on your body?

Take your right hand and rub the back of your left hand (You can use any action you prefer – I'm just using an example). FEEL the happiness.

Was that hard? What we have done was to anchor that feeling of happiness. Next time you are starting to feel not so good (and that is usually the result of your thoughts), just rub your right hand on your left hand. Your mind will make the connection, because you have anchored the feeling. You will immediately start to feel better (provided of course that you are aware of your thoughts and you change the thoughts or your attention).

If you start to live more consciously, you'll be much happier. Worries only come from past tense or future tense. Something that had happened or something that is going to happen. In the present moment there can be no worries – and if you do, you are back into the future tense!

To summarise, your dominant energy vibration will increase by focussing on more positive things. This will result in good circumstances of the same energy vibration to be attracted into your life.

All of these pieces form part of the whole. Change your life style and it will change your dominant energy vibration.

You need to get active, become healthy and fit, eat healthy foods and feel better. Depression is a low vibration energy you want to avoid at all cost. Clear your head of all those unnecessary worries and angry thoughts.

You'll be surprised how circumstances automatically change in your life for the better. It's almost like going to the water park and climbing in a super tube. You need to do something on your part (climbing in the super tube), but once the stream of water takes you, you are in for a fun ride! You don't do anything, you just enjoy the ride.

6. CONCLUSION

Money is energy, just like you. If you don't have enough of it in your life, it is an indication that there are energy blockages. One of the characteristics of money energy is that it flows. It is suppose to flow to you and then to the next person and to the next.

It may be that the money energy is flowing to you, but there are certain blockages that prevent it from manifesting in your life. These blockages are usually limiting beliefs. Sometimes a persons' dominant energy vibration is on such a low level that the person is not even attracting money energy.

Getting rid of energy clusters and clearing the energy in yourself and in your environment, as explained, should open the channels for the money energy to flow into your life. In very few cases the energy blockage can be so deep that the person will need an energy expert to help.

If you should take a pen and paper and write down what things are wrong in your life, you should be able to identify the limiting beliefs. Your life experience is a reflection (remember the mirror? ☺) of your inner self. This means that your limiting beliefs will be reflected in your life experience.

Being aware of these beliefs will make a difference already. Give reasons to yourself why your belief is not true and it should be enough to get rid of that belief. Unfortunately, beliefs that are almost the same tend to flock together. You need to identify a whole bunch of them in order to have your overall dominant energy vibration raised.

Learn to control and focus your mind. Your mind is the biggest cause of your stress. You cannot raise your dominant energy vibration if you are living a stressful live. If you focus on the negative then that is what you'll see.

The problem with stress is that you are not aware of it 95% of the time. Uncontrolled, limiting thoughts create this tension in your body. Muscles will contract and the flow of manifesting energy will be blocked. People only become aware of the stress when it manifests in the form of a physical illness or pain. The sad thing is that when we eventually become aware of our stressful ways, we don't have a clue how deep and serious the situation really is.

It is time to relax. Let go and let God.

Use your common sense when it comes to money and believe in yourself. Get your dominant energy vibration high, avoid negative energy and enjoy life!

The funny thing is that the moment your energy raises, new money making ideas will pop up in your mind. Act on them, because the money energy is knocking on your door! Before long you'll be wondering why you have struggled for so long. Everything will just seem to fall into place. The answer will seem so simplistic....and it always is. People tend to make things to difficult for themselves and they over complicate everything.

It will be much appreciated if you can tell me your success story after applying these principles. Just let me know at info@subconsciousbeliefs.com.
You may just be in my next book!

If you want to know more about the spiritual principles of abundance, get my book Subconscious Beliefs. If you want to know more about your mindset and finances, you can read A Poor Man's Journey.

May the riches be with you!

And remember....

The follow up book is NOW available!

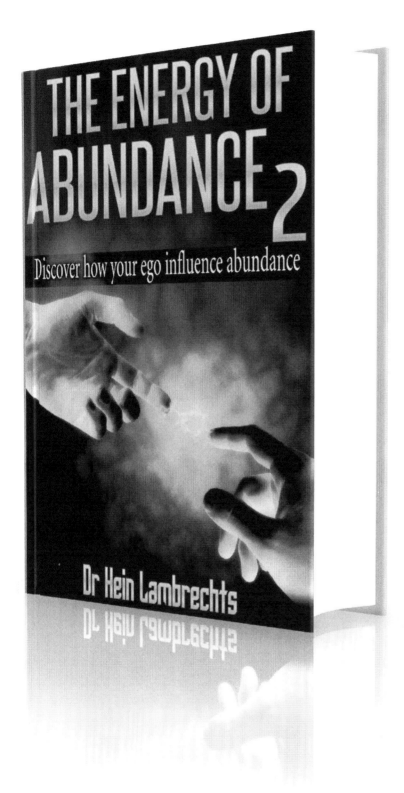

THE ENERGY OF ABUNDANCE 2

Discover how your ego influence abundance

Dr Hein Lambrechts

Made in the USA
Las Vegas, NV
01 July 2021